E
1957

The Top News
Stories of the Year

By Hugh Morrison

Montpelier Publishing
London

ISBN-13: 978-1975908928
ISBN-10: 1975908929
Published by Montpelier Publishing, London.
Printed and distributed by Amazon Createspace.

Image credits: Arpingstone, Associated Press, Calflier, Eiganotomo,
Echetuxe, Toni Frissell, Geni, Warren K Leffler/Library of Congress,
Erling Mandelmann, Chris Newman, Tom Palumbo, Mike Peel/University
of Manchester, Peeperman, Abbie Rowe, David Scanlan, Gregory R Todd
Katherine Young/German Federal Archive

Events of
1957

'You've never had it so good'

Harold MacMillan becomes Prime Minister

Harold MacMillan (1894-1986) took over from Anthony Eden as Britain's Prime Minister on 9 January 1957.

Britain had been humiliated in its forced withdrawal from the Suez Canal the previous year, and many blamed Eden, who finally resigned on grounds of ill-health.

A 'one nation Tory' (Conservative), MacMillan promoted full employment and industrial development, which lead to a boom in Britain's economy. Coupled with this were increases in benefits and reductions in working hours,

leading him to make in a 1957 speech his famous slogan, 'You've never had it so good.'

In 1958 a cartoonist parodied him as Superman and nicknamed him 'Supermac,' but the parody backfired and the nickname was taken up by his supporters.

MacMillan went on to lead the Conservatives to victory in the 1959 General Election. A series of scandals, however, most notably the Profumo Affair of 1963, led to his popularity dropping and his replacement by Foreign Secretary Alec Douglas-Home in September of that year.

Play it again, Sam

Film legend Humphrey Bogart dies aged 56

Play it again, Sam – probably one of the best known lines in movie history, is attributed to Humphrey Bogart in *Casablanca* (1942). However, Bogart never actually said it – the oft-misquoted line was in fact 'You played it for her, you can play it for me.'

Humphrey Bogart, despite his tough-guy persona, was born into a well-to-do New York family; he served in WW1 in the US Navy where he received the injury to his upper lip which helped give him his distinctive lisp.

Bogart's acting career began on the stage but he soon made the transition to the 'talkies' and was featured in many gangster and crime dramas of the 1930s. He shot to stardom in 1942 with wartime romance *Casablanca* and in the post war period began to make more serious, nuanced pictures including *The Caine Mutiny* as well as lighter films such as *The African Queen*. He is also famous for co-starring with his future wife, Lauren Bacall, in 1945's *To Have and Have Not*.

A lifelong heavy smoker and drinker, Bogart's health began to worsen and he was diagnosed with terminal cancer. He died on 13 January 1957 after a long decline, but cinematically, went out on a high: his final film, the boxing drama *The Harder They Fall* (1956) is one of his best.

Operation Power Flite

USAF shows global supremacy

Three B-52 bombers from the Power Flite mission

The US Air Force demonstrated to the world on 18 January 1957 that it was capable of dropping a hydrogen bomb anywhere in the world, with a record breaking non-stop global flight of five B-52 bombers.

The mission, led by Maj Gen Archie J Old, involved five bombers of the USAF 15th Air Force. They began the trip from Castle Air Force base in California on 16 January. Refueling in mid-air, the planes crossed the Atlantic and north Africa then travelled via India to Malaya where they made a simulated bombing drop.

Finally the convoy crossed the Pacific and landed at March Air Force base in California. The mission took 45 hours and 19 minutes to traverse 24,325 miles; less than half the time of the previous non-stop circumnavigation which took place in 1949.

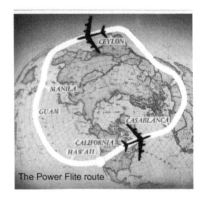

The Power Flite route

Third time lucky for Liz?

Elizabeth Taylor marries Mike Todd

In February 1957 Hollywood sensation Elizabeth Taylor married theatre and film producer Mike Todd. It was the third of her eight marriages but marred by tragedy; of all her marriages it was the only one ended by death, when Todd was killed in a plane accident just over a year later.

Todd (real name Avrom Goldbogen) had previously been married to actress Joan Blondell and was best known in Hollywood for directing the Academy Award winning 1956 picture *Around the World in Eighty Days* and for developing the 70mm Todd-AO widescreen cinema format.

In August 1957 the couple had a daughter, Elizabeth Frances.

In 1958, Todd flew by private plane from Los Angeles to New York. En route to an awards ceremoney, Taylor was due to accompany him but was unable to due to illness. The plane suffered engine failure and crashed in New Mexico killing all onboard. The only item of Todd's recovered was his wedding ring.

Below: Liz Taylor in 1957
Left: Todd and Taylor in an advertisement for TWA airlines.

Emergency Ward 10

Forerunner of medical soaps such as *Casualty*

Ask people today what was Britain's first TV soap opera and most will probably say *Coronation Street*, which started in 1960. But there are one or two earlier contenders, most notably 1957's hospital drama serial *Emergency Ward 10*.

Set in the fictional Oxbridge General Hospital, the serial followed the professional and private lives of doctors and nurses, with inevitable romantic entanglements.

Originally intended as a short run serial only called *Calling Nurse Roberts*, the show's popularity with viewers led to it becoming a permanent fixture on the schedules for ten years.

Soap operas often lead the way in reflecting (some might say influencing as well) changing social attitudes, and *Emergency* was a notable example when it featured an inter-racial love affair between a British doctor and a West Indian surgeon (played by Joan Hooley, who went on to play Josie McFarlane in BBC's *Eastenders*). This was a step too far in the conservative atmosphere of the day, and Hooley's character was soon written out of the show, by being sent to Africa where she died from a snakebite.

When ratings began to decline, legendary producer Lew Grade decided to change the show to a weekly one-hour episode, which failed to save the programme, although the format was revived in the 1970s with *General Hospital*, and paved the way for other long running medical dramas such as *Casualty*.

Emergency Ward 10's surviving episodes were released on DVD by Network in 2008.

Hit for Holly

The Crickets release *That'll Be the Day*

One of the best-selling singles of all time, *That'll be the Day* was written by Buddy Holly and Jerry Allison. Initially released in 1956 by Buddy Holly and the Three Tunes, it was re-released the following year by Holly with his new band, the Crickets.

Thought to be inspired by the John Wayne film *The Searchers* in which Wayne's catchphrase was 'that'll be the day,' the song peaked at number one in the UK singles chart in November 1957 and stayed there for three weeks.

Re-released in 1969, the song went on to be billed at number 39 on Rolling Stone's 500 greatest hits of all time. Other versions were popular too: Linda Rondstat's 1976 version reached number 11 in the US charts.

In a way that Holly could never have conceived at the time, a version of the song has become one of the most valuable records ever produced. John Lennon's first

group, the Quarrymen, which later evolved into the Beatles, recorded the song as a demonstration disc. Eventually released on a compilation album in the 90s, the original pressing is thought to be worth in the region of £100,000.

Buddy Holly was killed in a plane crash in 1959 along with other performers including Ritchie Valens and J.P. Richardson (the 'Big Bopper'making the final lines of the song, 'That'll be the day when I die' all the more evocative.

Queen of the *King and I*

Deborah Kerr wins Golden Globe

Deborah Kerr.
Right: Yul Brynner.

Scottish-born actress Deborah Kerr (1921-2007) received a Golden Globe in 1957 for her part in the hit musical film *The King and I,* released the previous year.

The film is based on the memoirs of Anna Leonowens (1831-1915), a British governess sent to tutor the children of the King of Siam (now Thailand).

The film's plot revolves around the clash of eastern and western culture and the battle of wills between the King and the confident, assertive Anna. The film featured songs such as *Getting To Know You* and *Shall We Dance?* which went on to become hits, although Kerr herself did not sing – her voice was dubbed by Marni Nixon.

The film also brought to the public's attention actor Yul Brynner who played the King. He shaved his head for the role and continued to do so for the rest of his life, becoming the first romantic Hollywood leading man with such a hairstyle.

Ghana goes its own way

Independence for British west African colony

The independence of India in 1947 started the long process of Britain's withdrawal from its Empire. The first candidate for independence among Britain's possessions in Africa was the colony of Gold Coast, which had been calling for self-rule since the establishment of the political body the United Gold Coast Convention in 1947.

Leader Kwame Nkrumah led the campaign with his slogan 'self government now'. On 6 March 1957 at 12.00 am Nkrumah was declared Prime Minister of Ghana. Following a referendum in 1960, the country became a Commonwealth Republic with Nkrumah as President.

Despite a series of political upheavals over the following years Ghana was relatively prosperous and became known as 'Africa's Success Story'.

Above: President Kwame Nkrumah 1909-1972.

Left: British Gold Coast stamp overlaid with Ghana independence marking.

Death in the Pacific

Phillipines president killed in plane crash

The Phillipines was plunged into mourning on 17 March 1957 as news spread of the death of Ramon del Fierro Magsaysay Sr, President of the Phillipines, in a plane crash. En route from Manila to Cebu City, the President's plane crash-landed on Mount Managgal with only one survivor, journalist Néstor Mata.

A former guerilla fighter against the Japanese during the islands' occupation, Magsaysay rose to power in the post war era and became a popular leader with staunch anti-communist Roman Catholic views, of particular appeal to the population of the only major Christian country in south-east Asia.

Early in his presidency he published the Magsaysay Credo outlining the principles for those holding high office. The final principle, which is inscribed on his tomb in Manila, is as follows:

'I believe that the President should set the example of a big heart, an honest mind, sound instincts, the virtue of healthy impatience, and an abiding love for the common man'.

Ramon Magsaysay, (1907-1957), the popular Phillipines President killed in a plane crash.

Sole survivor Néstor Mata later published his account of the crash, *One Came Back*.

First steps to European Union

The Treaty of Rome is signed

Politicians at the signing in the *Palazzo dei Conservatori*

On 25 March 1957 the first step towards the modern European Union took place with the signing of the Treaty of Rome, officially known as the 'Treaty Establishing the European Economic Community' (EEC).

The treaty, signed at the *Palazzo dei Conservatori* in the Italian capital, brought together France, West Germany, Italy, Belgium, Luxembourg, and the Netherlands in an agreement to reduce duty on goods and establish a customs union, with the eventual goal of a single common market. The treaty also paved the way for more idealistic plans for the future of the countries of Europe, including political union and a single currency, and helped shape the modern European Union.

Britain's attitude to European union has always been somewhat ambivalent and at the time of the Treaty it was felt by many that Britain's trade should be with Commonwealth rather than European countries. Britain eventually joined the EEC in 1973.

All change please

New York's last trolley car service ends

A PCC-type streetcar in New York in the last days of the trolley cars.

Trolley cars (trams or streetcars) first ran in New York City as early as the 1832 when they were pulled by horses. As the city became electrified in the late nineteenth century, the trolley car entered its golden age with a network of routes across the city.

Named after the 'trawler' which connected the car to the overhead power supply, the 'trolley' soon became a familiar sight and popular way to get around. After WW1 competition grew in the form of cars and buses, which could not use the dedicated trolley lines. Following lobbying by auto manufacturers and oil companies, trollies began to go into decline and were gradually replaced by bus services. The last streetcar ran from Queens to Manhattan on 6 April 1957. The service was largely unlamented and its facilities were boarded up and forgotten.

The trolley car may, however, have the last laugh. In 2016 proposals were made by New York's mayor to reinstate services on some routes in order to beat congestion.

End of the end of the pier show

Laurence Olivier stars in *The Entertainer.*

Following the smash hit of his 1956 play *Look Back in Anger*, 'angry young man' playwright John Osborne had another success with 1957's *The Entertainer.*

Starring theatre legend Laurence Olivier as Archie Rice, the play uses the format of the dying music hall/end of pier (vaudeville) tradition to examine Britain's post-imperial role, and in particular its relationship with the USA.

Writing in the Observer, critic Kenneth Tynan stated 'Mr Osborne has had the big and brilliant notion of putting the whole of contemporary England onto one and the same stage ... He chooses, as his national microcosm, a family of run-down vaudevillians.'

The play was a huge success, starting at the Royal Court Theatre in London on 10 April and then touring the provinces, with a US tour in 1958. Revivals were held in 1974, 1986, 2007 and 2016, with

Laurence Olivier and Joan Plowright

the '74 show featuring genuine music hall performer Max Wall.

The Entertainer was prescient: Britain's last major chain of music halls closed in 1960 and in 1963, one of its last great stars, Max Miller (upon whom the character of Rice was partly based) died, marking the end of the tradition that Osborne had predicted just three years before.

Singapore goes it alone

British colony opts for independence

Pro-Chinese demonstration in post-war Singapore. The British authorities were concerned about a communist takeover.

Following Ghana's independence earlier in the year, the next stop on Britain's long withdrawal from Empire was its colony of Singapore in the Malay peninsula.

Under British control since the early 19th century, the island was the scene of Britain's largest military defeat when in 1942 130,000 troops surrendered to the invading Japanese forces, who occupied the territory for three years.

Britain's failure to defend Singapore was probably a significant factor in the postwar push for independence, and moves towards self-government began with elections in 1948. Progress, led by Chief Minister David Marshall was slow, however, with the British concerned that the island could fall under the influence of the communists fighting a guerilla war in nearby Malaya.

In March 1957 a formal agreement was made for self-government to begin in 1958, under the leadership of Chief Minister Lim Yew Hock. Despite a shaky start, independent Singapore went on to become in the 1960s an economic powerhouse under Lee Kuan Yew, known as the 'founder of modern Singapore.

Court in the act

Legal drama *12 Angry Men* released

The 1950s are known as a conservative era, but a number of films of the time hinted towards the more liberal attitudes of the following decade. One such example is Reginald Rose's courtroom drama *12 Angry Men* starring Henry Fonda and directed by Sidney Lumet.

The film, released on 13 April 1957, is based in the jury room of a court as the twelve men have to reach a verdict in a case where their decision will mean life or death for the defendant.

Consensus is built with difficulty, as the men have differing views on capital punishment and there are several clashes of personality; the pressure builds and it is not until the last minute an unanimous verdict is reached.

The film, rehearsed in only three weeks and produced on a minimal budget of $340,000, was well received but did not do particularly well at the box office.

The claustrophobic setting lent itself more to the small screen (a TV version had been broadcast in 1954), and it was on television that the film found greater success, gaining new fans with each successive generation.

In 2011 the film was reported as the second most often shown in British schools, presumably because of its depiction of the workings of the common-law jury system.

Dawn of the *Sky at Night*

First episode of long running BBC series

The Sky At Night, the BBC's monthly astronomy programme, was first broadcast on 25 April 1957 with presenter Sir Patrick Moore CBE. Moore hosted the programme until his death in 2012, making it the world's longest running TV show with the same presenter.

Moore, a former RAF pilot and amateur astronomer, had a unique eccentric presentation style with a dishevelled appearance and trademark monocle in his right eye. This was no gimmick, however: when it came to explaining complex matters of astronomy Moore was able to explain things in layman's terms in a straightforward way, helping him to become one of Britain's most popular TV presenters. Since his death the programme has continued with other presenters, most notably Brian May, former guitarist with Queen.

The programme has had the same highly recognisable theme tune since its inception: *At The Castle Gate* by Sibelius.

Flying Officer Sir Patrick Moore CBE in later life.

Profiles in Courage

Future US president releases book

In 1957 future US President,(at that time Senator for Massachusetts) John F Kennedy published *Profiles in Courage.*

The book, which went on to win a Pulitzer Prize, is a collection of biographical essays on a number of US politicians of the nineteenth and twentieth centuries who spoke out against popular opinion, in particular those who attempted to prevent the outbreak of the Civil War.

The book also looks at more recent politicians such as George Norris who opposed US involvement in the First World War and Robert A. Taft who criticised the conduct of the Nuremberg Trials.

The book became an instant bestseller, and, following Kennedy's assassination in 1963, returned to the bestseller lists. It was also made into a TV series by NBC in 1964.

Questions, however, have arisen over how much input Kennedy had into the book. Following the award of the Pulitzer Prize for the book, journalist Drew Pearson claimed on CBS TV that it had largely been ghost-written, but the station later retracted the statement. The book remains in print to this day.

Full time for Stanley Matthews

Legendary footballer plays final game for England

Sir Stanley Matthews CBE (1915-2000), a professional footballer since 1930, played his final game for England on 15 May 1957, when at 42 years of age he became the oldest player to represent the country, in a World Cup qualifier against Denmark.

Matthews continued, however, to play at club level, and did not finally retire from professional football until aged 50 in 1965, when he also became the only footballer to be knighted while still a professional player. A successful career in coaching followed and he played his last amateur game in 1985 at the age of 70.

Matthews was a hugely popular player with his fans; his biographer Les Scott described how he could 'sprinkle gold dust on their harsh working lives.'

At his funeral in his native town of Stoke-on-Trent, 100,000 people lined the streets to pay tribute, and a statue was erected outside the town's Britannia Stadium in his memory.

Stanley Matthews at the 1953 FA Cup Final.

Statue in Stoke.

Britain goes nuclear

H-Bomb tests in the Pacific

Left: hydrogen bomb explodes at Christmas Island. Above: the RAF Vickers Valiant.

Operation Grapple was the codename for a series of atomic weapons tests carried out by Britain in 1957.

Britain had begun a nuclear weapons research programme in the early 1940s, with a successful test of an atom bomb in 1952. By 1957 they were ready to test the far more powerful thermonuclear or hydrogen bomb.

This took place in May and June 1957 at Malden Island in the Pacific. The first bomb was dropped from a Vickers Valiant aircraft by Wing Commander Kenneth Hubbard of the RAF.

Further testing took place on Christmas Island later in the year and into 1958, when a moratorium was put into place.

By then it was confirmed that Britain was a global nuclear power, leading to the 1958 US-UK Mutual Defence Agreement, today part of the two countries' longstanding security arrangements known as the Special Relationship.

The great Crusader

Billy Graham holds biggest ever rally

Evangelist Billy Graham (1918-) had held a series of religious missions ('Crusades') in various locations since 1947. In 1957 he held his biggest yet, with a 16-week run at New York's Madison Square Garden, with 18,000 people attending.

The sessions consisted of choral music, a sermon and prayers by Graham and then the famous 'altar call' where attendees would be invited to come forward as a sign of dedication of their lives to Christ.

Although Graham was a popular, charismatic preacher; with considerable personal appeal, the rally was helped by a huge public relations campaign on billboards, on TV and in newspapers, with the New York Times printing his sermons in full. This sealed Graham's reputation as probably the best known evangelical preacher of the twentieth century.

Earning with ERNIE

HM Treasury launches supercomputer

The original ERNIE computer

ERNIE moneybox

Launched in 1956 by the UK government the Premium Bond was an innovative savings vehicle. Investors bought bonds which were 100% secure as they were backed by the Treasury. No interest was paid, but each bond was entered into a monthly lottery to win a cash prize.

This was largely due to social disapproval of gambling (unlike most countries Britain had no national lottery until 1994); although prizes might be won, the 'stake' was retained.

In 1957 the government introduced ERNIE (Electronic Random Number Indicator Equipment), an enormous computer which selected the winning numbers. ERNIE was based on Colossus, the world's first digital computer. Although computers had been used by the government in secret in the Second World War, ERNIE was the first widely publicised computer to be used in civilian life in the UK.

The British public, unfamiliar with the idea of computers or what they looked like, attributed human characteristics to ERNIE; it received letters and Christmas cards and was even made the subject of a pop song by 1980s group Madness.

ERNIE's descendant, ERNIE 4, is the size of a standard personal computer and has been in use since 2004.

My Way – not yours

Frank Sinatra and Ava Gardner divorce

Frank Sinatra (1915-1998) separated from his first wife Nancy Barbado in 1950, following a tempestuous affair with actress and singer Ava Gardner (1922-1990). In 1951 Sinatra and Gardner were married in Las Vegas, Nevada.

According to Sinatra's unauthorised biography *His Way* by Kitty Kelley, Gardner at first detested Sinatra but grew to like him through discovering a mutual love of hard drinking and sports.

The marriage however was turbulent, with well publicised fights and arguments, culminating with the couple formally announcing their separation on 29 October 1953.

The divorce case, begun in 1954 took three years to settle with Sinatra reportedly profoundly depressed by it. Sinatra, however, continued to manage Gardner's money until 1976, and assisted her financially when she became ill in later life.

Fete lends a hand

Lennon and McCartney's first meeting

One of music's most historic meetings took place in the grounds of the church of St Peter, Woolton, Liverpool, on 6 July 1957, when 16 year old John Lennon met 15 year old Paul McCartney at the church's annual garden fete.

Lennon was performing at the fete with his skiffle band, The Quarrymen, formed the previous year and named after his school, Quarry Bank.

McCartney was introduced to Lennon by his friend Ivan Vaughan, the Quarrymen's bass player. McCartney showed Lennon how to tune a guitar and then played a few rock and roll songs with the band. The pair became friends and went on to form the Beatles in 1960.

Remarkably, this first performance was recorded on reel-to-reel tape, which was auctioned at Sotheby's in 1994 for £78,500, at that time the most expensive recording sold at auction.

The churchyard of St Peter's is also notable for containing the grave of one Eleanor Rigby, (1895-1939) who inspired the Beatles song of the same name.

End of the Bey

Tunisia's last monarch deposed

One of history's shortest-lived monarchies came to an end in 1957 as the Kingdom of Tunisia was declared a Republic, and its king, Muhammed VIII, deposed.

Tunisia had been a French protectorate since 1881, but was granted independence in 1956 as part of a general retreat of the French from their North African possessions. Originally the French had intended home rule for Tunisia with a continuing military presence, but troops were required to keep order in neighbouring Algeria.

Pan-Arab nationalists seized the opportunity to press for full sovereignty, and in March 1956 the country became a constitutional monarchy with King Muhammed VIII as head of state.

Muhammed was one of long line of Beys of Tunis, a form of king dating from the era of the Ottoman Empire in the eighteenth century. The Beys however were considered by

HM King Muhammad VIII of Tunisia

nationalists to be puppets of the French empire and the institution was opposed by nationalist prime minister Habib Ben Ali Bourguiba.

In 1957 Bourguiba abolished the monarchy and became President of a one-party state, eventually declaring himself President for Life in 1975, eventually being deposed himself in 1987.

If the Capp fits...

Lovable cartoon layabout makes first appearance

Capp with his long suffering wife Flo

Statue in Hartlepool

The *Daily Mirror* newspaper launched a new comic character on 5 August 1957: workshy northern layabout Andy Capp.

Based in Hartlepool in north east England, Andy is a hard drinking, gambling workshy layabout, persistently cadging money off his longsuffering wife Flo and having run-ins with local authority figures including the rent collector, the vicar and the police.

The 'lovable rogue' character in a familiar northern working class setting was a hit with British readers as well as worldwide, and Andy has continued to appear in the *Daily Mirror* to this day, despite the death of his creator, Reg Smyth, in 1998.

Over the years Andy has made numerous appearances in addition to newspapers, including a TV series, an animated cartoon, TV advertisements and a stage musical. A children's comic, *Buster: Son of Andy Capp* ran from 1960 to 2000.

The character is also known in the USA on a range of snack foods, 'Andy Capp's Fries', and in Australia there was even a chain of off-licences named after him!

Last laugh

Comedy legend Oliver Hardy dies

The world of comedy lost one of its legends on 7 August 1957 with the death of Oliver Norvell Hardy at the age of 65.

His death brought to an end the comic institution that was Laurel and Hardy.

The son of a Confederate Civil War veteran, Hardy went into acting at a young age, working as a singer and comedian on the vaudeville (music hall) circuit in Jacksonville, Florida.

Although Hardy is best known for his partnership with Stan Laurel (1890-1965), he began as a solo performer, appearing in over 200 comedy films before making his first with Laurel in 1921.

Hal Roach Studios noticed how well audiences reacted to them and the pair went on to make over 100 films together until their final feature, *Atoll K,* in 1950.

In his last years Hardy went on a stage tour around the United Kingdom with Laurel to meet British fans; they were received like royalty with huge crowds turning out to see them; a fitting end to an illustrious career.

Independence for Malaya

'Good Year Has Come To Us'

Another jewel in Britain's imperial crown was removed in 1957 as the colony of the Federation of Malaya became an independent state within the Commonwealth.

The Federation, a collection of states in the Malayan Peninsula which included Malacca and Penang, had gradually come under British control over the course of the eighteenth and nineteenth centuries.

Against a backdrop of guerilla war against communist insurgents (the Malayan Emergency), the handover of power took place on 31 August at Merdeka Stadium in the capital, Kuala Lumpur, where the Queen's representative HRH the Duke of Gloucester formally handed control to Prime Minister-designate Tunku Abdul Rahman.

Malaysian Mufti Syeikh Abdullah Fahim declared in Arabic 'good year has come to us!'

British and Commonwealth troops continued fighting against guerillas in Malaya until 1960 when the communists surrendered.

Statue of Captain Francis Light, founder of the British colony of Penang

Commonwealth troops on patrol in the Malayan Emergency

The beat of a generation

Beatnik novel *On the Road* published

Counter-culture is often thought to have started in the 1960s, but its origins were earlier, with the Beat Generation (or Beatniks) – the 1950s forerunners of the hippies.

A seminal text for the Beats was Jack Kerouac's *On the Road*, published in September 1957. The book is a semi-autobiographical account of Kerouac's alcohol and drug-fueled road trips across the USA and Mexico with other Beats such as Alan Ginsberg and William S Burroughs.

Born in 1922, Kerouac briefly served in the US Navy but was discharged on psychiatric grounds and drifted into writing, publishing a series of books with varying success from 1950. An opponent of communism, Kerouac did not win many friends on the left, but nor did his drug use and sexual exploits endear him to the conservative right.

His writing contains philosophical and religious themes, centering around Roman Catholicism and Buddhism, with the latter perhaps influencing the eastern mysticism that pervaded the hippy culture of the 1960s.

On the Road assured Kerouac a place in the American literary canon but later works failed to gain as much popularity with fans. Kerouac died of alcohol-related illness in 1969, aged 47.

The 'Old Man' is back

West Germany re-elects Adenauer

One of the world's oldest democratically elected statesmen, Konrad Adenauer, known in Germany as 'Der Alte' (the 'Old Man') was re-elected to serve as Chancellor of West Germany in 1957.

Adenauer (1876-1967) was a career politician from a young age; exempted from military service on health grounds he was vice-Mayor of Cologne during the Great War and maintained order during the Bolshevik uprising and subsequent British occupation of the Rhineland in 1919.

A devout Roman-Catholic and anti-communist, Adenauer had strong dislike of the Nazi party as it gained power in the 1930s. In 1933 he was dismissed as Mayor and withdrew from public life. By 1944, plans were in place to deport him to a concentration camp but friends were able to save him by having him admitted to hospital.

Following the Allied occupation in 1945, Adenauer's status as an anti-Nazi enabled him to once again climb the political ladder and he was elected Chancellor in 1949, a position he was to hold until 1963.

Adenauer's lasting legacy is of having helped transform West Germany from its pre-1945 authoritarianism to an economically successful modern democratic state.

Love without borders

Sophie Loren and Carlo Ponti banned from Italy

'It would be impossible to love anyone else'. So said film star Sophie Loren of her husband Carlo Ponti when speaking of her fifty-year marriage; a marriage that took 11 years and a change of nationality to be recognised.

Loren (born 1934) was just beginning to come to the public's notice by the mid 1950s and had appeared in several films in Italy and the USA. During this time she met and fell in love with producer Carlo Ponti. Ponti, however, was married with two children and divorce at the time was illegal in Italy. Eventually he was able to obtain a divorce in Mexico and marry Loren in 1957, but the Italian authorities made it clear that if they returned to Italy from the USA Ponti would be charged with bigamy.

Thus began a complicated legal battle and eventually the couple had to become French citizens in order for their marriage to finally be recognised in 1966. They remained together until Ponti's death in 2007.

Legal Eagle

Raymond Burr stars as Perry Mason

1957 saw the TV debut of Erle Stanley Gardner's fictional defence lawyer Perry Mason, played by Raymond Burr (1917-1993).

The *Perry Mason* TV show was an adaptation of a series of novels by Erle Stanley Gardner (1889-1970) which had already been successfully adapted for the big screen and the radio in the 1930s and 1940s.

It was apparent that television, with its close-ups and narrow camera angles, was the perfect medium for tense courtroom drama and the series became incredibly popular, with writers adapting all of Gardner's works and adding new stories when the original stock was exhausted.

The series ran until 1966 with worldwide syndication and repeats, with a less successful remake in the 1970s. Burr received two Emmy Awards for the role, and went on to play another famous crime fighter, the wheelchair bound detective *Ironside*.

The 'People's King'

Olav V becomes King of Norway

Following the death of his father Haakon VII on 21 September 1957, Olav V (born 1903) became King of Norway.

Known as the 'People's King', Olav reigned in a style familiar to us now as the 'Scandinavian Model', driving his own car, cycling and using public transport. When asked how he managed without bodyguards, he said 'I have four million bodyguards,' – the population of Norway at the time.

Olav continued the close links between the British and Norwegian monarchies. Descended from Queen Victoria and born at Sandringham, England, he was educated at Oxford and along with his father he represented the Norwegian government in exile in Britain during the Second World War.

He died in 1991 and was succeeded by his son Harald V, the present King of Norway.

Olav V

Haakon VII

Big trouble in Little Rock

Protestors oppose racial desegregation in schools

Troops escort black pupils into Central High School, Little Rock

Known as the Little Rock Nine, a group of American high school pupils made history on 4 September 1957 as they became the first black children to attend the recently desegrated Central High School in Little Rock, Arkansas.

Racial segregation of schools throughout the USA had been outlawed by Congress in 1954 and by 1957, with help from the National Association for the Advancement of Colored People (NAACP) the first nine black pupils had been enrolled at Central. Protestors opposed to desegregation picketed the school, however, and in an attempt to keep the peace (or to prevent desegregation; the motive remains unclear) the state governor Orval Faubus ordered troops from the National Guard to prevent the black pupils entering.

Photos of the event shocked the nation and President Eisenhower ordered the National Guard of the state to be brought under federal control. Troops were eventually used to escort the Little Rock Nine to school, although disturbances and harrassment of black pupils continued for a long time afterwards.

Crossing into Hell

The Bridge on the River Kwai is released

Right: Alec Guinness
as Lt Col Nicholson

David Lean's epic and moving war drama *The Bridge on the River Kwai* was released in October 1957.

It is a fictional account of the construction of a bridge on the infamous Burma Road by prisoners of the Japanese during the Second World War.

In the film, the allied prisoners work as slowly as possible, deliberately trying to sabotage construction of the bridge. The senior British officer, Lt Col Nicholson (Alec Guinness) becomes convinced that a proper job must be done, in order to show the Japanese that his men have skill and self-respect and are not merely sub-human slaves.

The other soldiers view Nicholson as a collaborator, and in the final scene, while attempting to prevent the destruction of the bridge by hidden mines, he is shot by one of his own men and the bridge is blown up.

The film was widely acclaimed and won seven Academy Awards.

Journey into space

Sputnik I is first manmade object in orbit

Although rockets had been sent into near-space by the Germans during the Second World War, the Soviet Union was the first country to successfully launch an object into orbit around earth.

Sputnik I, a metal sphere 23 inches in diameter with three aerials, was launched by rocket from Kazakhstan on 4 October 1957 and orbited the earth at 18,000mph, taking 96 minutes to complete each circuit. Radio signals with a distinctive 'beep' sound were broadcast to earth and picked up by amateur radio enthusiasts worldwide; the satellite was also just visible to the naked eye at night.

The launch was a huge propaganda coup for the USSR, and set in motion the 'space race' between the two rival countries.

Sputnik I fell to earth in January 1958.

Artist's impression of Sputnik I in orbit.

Great Balls of Fire

Two smash hits in one year for Jerry Lee Lewis

In 1957 rock and roll singer Jerry Lee Lewis shot to fame with two smash hits in the year: *Whole Lotta Shakin' Goin' On* and *Great Balls of Fire*.

Whole Lotta Shakin' Goin' On had been recorded earlier by other artists but Lewis added his unique boogie-woogie piano playing and verbal asides to make it his own. The record hit the top of the charts and became a rock and roll classic with *Rolling Stone* magazine eventually rating it as the 61st best song of all time.

His next song, *Great Balls of Fire,* was another runaway hit, selling over five million copies, with a million sold in just the first ten days after release in the USA.

Great Balls of Fire became another classic and, most recently, has been used as the theme tune for WWE Wrestling on US TV.

Spotlight on the stars

World's largest telescope goes into operation

Jodrell Bank Observatory, near Manchester, England, started out in 1939 as a small research station with just a few wooden huts. In the post-war era it developed rapidly, and by 1957 work was complete on the Lovell Telescope, at the time the world's largest radio telescope. This was just in time for it to observe the launch of the Soviet satellite Sputnik I.

The telescope, which incorporated military surplus gun turret mechanisms in its design, was so powerful that both US and Soviet governments asked Jodrell Bank to make observations of their rocket launches. One notable example was the observation of the Russian unmanned moon landing in 1966, when Lovell was able to relay photographs taken by the Luna 9 landing module.

Although no longer the world's largest telescope, the Jodrell Bank site has expanded to include a visitor centre, an academic research station and several other large telescopes.

The Lovell Telescope. Inset: an early radio telescope at Jodrell Bank in 1945.

Queen of Canada

HM Queen Elizabeth II opens Parliament

Right: the Queen and Prince Philip arrive in Canada

Left: the Queen meets the 'Mounties'; the Royal Canadian Mounted Police.

History was made on 14 October 1957 when HM Queen Elizabeth II opened the Canadian Parliament.

Although her father, HM King George VI, had visited it in 1939, Parliament had never been opened by a reigning British sovereign since its establishment by the Crown in 1867. The function instead was, and is, carried out by the monarch's representative, the Governor General.

Large crowds gathered to greet the Queen and Prince Philip wherever they went, with around 50,000 people watching the arrival of the royal party at Parliament. The visit was also notable for including the Queen's first live televised address.

The visit helped reinforce the relationship between Canada and the UK, establishing a unique, more relaxed and modern style of monarchy.

Elvis on the inside

Elvis Presley stars in *Jailhouse Rock*

Produced quickly to capitalise on the growing appeal of rock singer Elvis Presley, the 1957 movie *Jailhouse Rock* nonetheless contains a number of good songs and a memorable dance sequence (shown above).

In the film, Presley plays Vince Everett, sent to the state penitentiary for accidentally killing a man in a barroom brawl. Everett is taught to play the guitar by a washed up country singer, Hunk Houghton, but following a televised talent show from the jail, Houghton becomes jealous of Everett's growing fame. Upon release from prison, Everett becomes a big star and falls in love with music promoter Peggy (played by Judy Tyler).

Houghton is later released and claims he is owed money because he taught Everett all he knows. He attacks Everett, who refuses to fight back and receives a blow to the throat.

At first it is thought Everett has lost his voice permanently, but he eventually recovers and the film ends with Everett singing another of the film's hits, *Young and Beautiful,* to Peggy.

Laika the Space Dog

Soviets send first animal into orbit

Laika was a stray mongrel dog found on the streets of Moscow who achieved worldwide fame by becoming the first animal to enter into earth orbit on the Sputnik II rocket on 3 November 1957.

Stray dogs were chosen because it was thought they were already adapted to harsh conditions. Laika was trained for the mission by keeping her in a series of capsules of decreasing size so that she would get used to confined spaces, as well as placing her on a centrifuge to get her used to zero gravity.

Readings showed that Laika survived the launch and was eating her food several hours into the flight. She was never intended to return to earth, as the technology for this did not exist, but was meant to be painlessly killed by poison gas when her food ran out. Readings suggested, however, that she probably died from overheating about seven hours into the flight.

Although it seemed cruel in some ways, Laika's mission greatly helped scientists enable Yuri Gagarin to travel safely into space four years later.

Left: the Sputnik II capsule in which Laika travelled.

Below: a Romanian stamp commemorating the mission.

BIRTHDAY NOTEBOOKS

FROM
MONTPELIER PUBLISHING

Handy 60-page ruled notebooks with a significant event of the year on each page.

A great alternative to a birthday card.
Available from Amazon.

Made in the USA
San Bernardino, CA
18 December 2019